THE BEATLES

A Little Golden Book® Biography

By Judy Katschke

Illustrated by Maike Plenzke

A GOLDEN BOOK • NEW YORK

Educators and librarians, for a variety of teaching tools, visit us at RHTeachersLibrarians.com
Library of Congress Control Number: 2022942360
ISBN 978-0-593-64512-3 (trade) — ISBN 978-0-593-64513-0 (ebook)
Printed in the United States of America
10 9 8 7 6 5 4 3 2 1

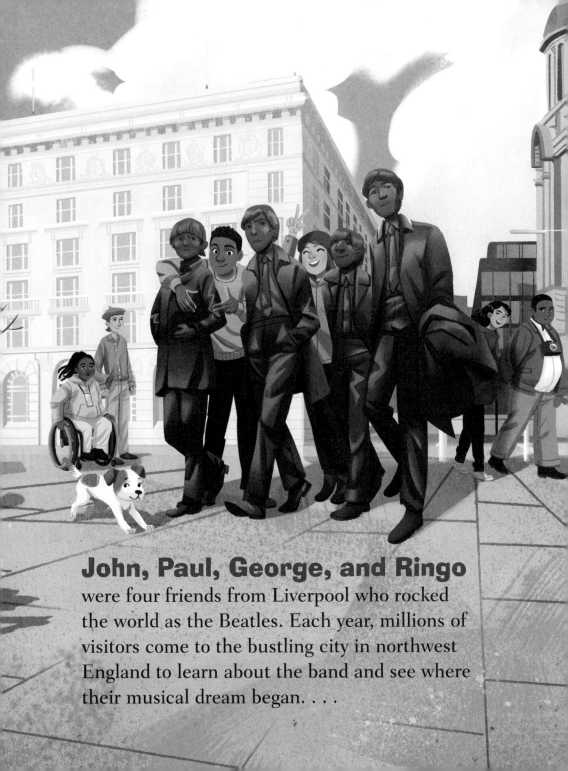

John, Paul, George, and Ringo were four friends from Liverpool who rocked the world as the Beatles. Each year, millions of visitors come to the bustling city in northwest England to learn about the band and see where their musical dream began. . . .

John Winston Lennon was born in Liverpool on October 9, 1940. His middle name came from England's prime minister at the time, Winston Churchill.

When John's parents split up, he went to live with his aunt Mimi. John spent hours in his room drawing cartoons, writing stories, and playing his guitar. The guitar was a gift from his mother, Julia, who died when he was seventeen.

Paul McCartney was born on June 18, 1942, into a house filled with music. His father was a cotton salesman who played piano and trumpet in his own jazz band. Paul turned down music lessons and instead taught himself how to play the piano and guitar.

Like John, Paul lost his mother when he was young. But John and Paul shared something else that would bring the two together—a love of music!

One summer day, Paul dropped by a festival to hear a band called the Quarrymen. Started by John, the Quarrymen played rock and roll music and jazzy tunes called skiffle. During the band's break, Paul played a few songs on the guitar. John liked what he heard and asked him to join the band.

The Quarrymen had kids dancing all over Liverpool. When they needed a third guitarist, Paul suggested his friend George Harrison.

Born on February 25, 1943, George fell in love with rock and roll after hearing Elvis Presley play "Heartbreak Hotel." When he got his first guitar, George practiced so much that his fingers were sore!

All that practice paid off! At the age of fifteen, George auditioned for the Quarrymen on the top of a double-decker bus. The band had found their new guitarist. Now all they needed was a new name.

One of the hottest groups at the time was the Crickets. John thought it would be cool for their band to have a bug name, too. Guitarist Stuart Sutcliffe suggested beetles or *beat*les. With their new name came a new goal: the Beatles would become famous. Or, as they liked to say, they'd go "to the toppermost of the poppermost!"

The Beatles were still far from famous when they were invited to perform in Hamburg, Germany. John, Paul, George, Stuart, and drummer Pete Best jumped at the chance to bring their tunes overseas. The band played every day of the week—sometimes for as long as eight hours!

After months of rocking Hamburg, the Beatles left Germany with new mop top haircuts, more fans, and their first recorded single, "My Bonnie." They also left without Stuart, who stayed in Hamburg to study art.

The Beatles were back in Liverpool and back to performing at small clubs. Fans stood wall-to-wall to hear them play. The band's popularity was growing. All they needed was a recording contract—and a little help from a friend named Brian Epstein.

As the Beatles' new manager, Brian got right to work. First, he changed the band's look. Instead of leather jackets and jeans, John, Paul, George, and Pete would perform in suits and ties. And the boys were expected to act like polite gentlemen and always be on time for their shows.

John and Paul got to work, too, teaming up to
write new songs. Paul wrote his lyrics neatly in
a notebook. John scribbled his songs on random
scraps of paper. Their writing styles were different,
but they led to catchy tunes such as "She Loves
You" and "I Want to Hold Your Hand."

The Beatles had great new songs but still no recording contract. Finally, a music producer named George Martin invited John, Paul, George, and Pete to audition at his studio. After hearing them play "Love Me Do," he offered the Beatles a contract and a suggestion: find a new drummer.

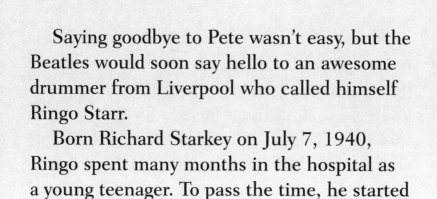

Saying goodbye to Pete wasn't easy, but the Beatles would soon say hello to an awesome drummer from Liverpool who called himself Ringo Starr.

Born Richard Starkey on July 7, 1940, Ringo spent many months in the hospital as a young teenager. To pass the time, he started drumming, grabbing whatever he could to bang on his bedside cabinet.

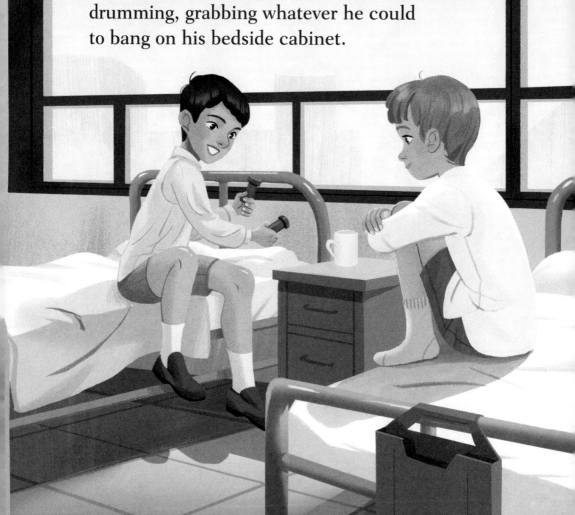

Years later, the drummer with many rings on his fingers had the right look—and the right beat—for the Beatles!

By 1963, Beatlemania had spread throughout England. Kids combed their Beatles haircuts, carried Beatles lunch boxes to school, and read Beatles magazines. When fans thought they knew the band's favorite candy, they showered the stage with jelly beans while they sang.

Along with the fame came a new nickname. John, Paul, George, and Ringo were called the Fab Four—because they were so fabulous!

BEATLE

The Beatles now sang at fancy London theaters—and even performed for the royal family! What could be bigger than that? Brian had an idea. The Beatles would go to America!

The first stop would be New York City to perform on a popular TV show. Then off to Washington, DC, for the first Beatles concert in the USA. To Brian's surprise, the Beatles were more worried than excited. Their song "I Want to Hold Your Hand" was a hit in America, but would they be?

On February 7, 1964, the Beatles arrived at New York's John F. Kennedy International Airport. The Fab Four didn't know what to expect until they were greeted by thousands of fans screaming their names and waving welcome signs. The Beatles had arrived in America—and so had Beatlemania!

That Sunday, seventy-three million Americans tuned in to meet the Beatles on the *Ed Sullivan Show*. In Washington, DC, they played in an arena packed with fans. John, Paul, George, and Ringo had truly reached the *toppermost of the poppermost*. And it was just the beginning. . . .

For the next six years, the Beatles would give the world over two hundred hit songs. They would be honored by their queen and star in five movies. The Beatles would become the best-selling band in music history. But through all their triumphs and fame, John, Paul, George, and Ringo would always be four friends from Liverpool who made their dreams come true!